SPIT, SCAREY ANN,
AND SWEAT BEES

SPIT, SCAREY ANN, AND SWEAT BEES

One Thing Leads To Another

KATHRYN TUCKER WINDHAM

NEWSOUTH BOOKS
Montgomery | Louisville

NewSouth Books
105 South Court Street
Montgomery, AL 36104

On the half title page, my baby photo, 1919

Library of Congress Cataloging-in-Publication
Data

Windham, Kathryn Tucker.
Spit, Scarey Ann, and sweat bees : one thing leads
to another / Kathryn Tucker Windham.
p. cm.
ISBN-13: 978-1-58838-240-5
ISBN-10: 1-58838-240-0
1. Windham, Kathryn Tucker—Childhood
and youth. 2. Thomasville (Ala.)—Biography. 3.
Thomasville (Ala.)—Social life and customs. I. Title.
F334.T48W57 2009
976.1'245—dc22
[B]

2009009232

Design by Randall Williams
Printed in the United States of America

For Thurza Hillery,

the only person who ever thought

I was perfect,

and for Thurza's daughter,

Bessie Gray Hillery,

the best playmate any little girl ever had.

— LIFE OF THE PARTY —

CONTENTS

Effie, my nurse

Outside my father's bank, Thomasville, 1919.

Superstitions

MY EARLIEST MEMORY IS OF BEING FRIGHTENED by a big grasshopper.

My nurse, Effie, was pushing me in my baby buggy, and as we crossed a soggy spot in the path to Effie's house, the green insect hopped on my coverlet, landing near my left hand. Effie quickly brushed the grasshopper away, but I had been terrorized.

It happened in the fall of 1920, soon after I turned two. Scoffers say I could not possibly remember such an early experience, but I do.

I don't know what brought that experience to mind; I haven't thought of it in years. Perhaps reading the Old Testament story about the plagues that Jehovah punished hard-hearted Pharaoh with, infestations of flies, lice, and locusts, stirred my memory.

Though I am not a Bible scholar (there have been long periods of time when I did not read it at all), some months ago our preacher suggested that we read the New Testament, two chapters a day. I followed his suggestion and, using a modern translation, I completed the assignment. I missed the beauty of the language in the King James version, but I did have a better understanding of what I read.

Then I decided to read the Old Testament, two chapters at a time. I have discovered stories, some tenderly romantic and some violently gory, that I had never known about before.

Certainly I had never been taught them in my Methodist Sunday school classes nor were they included in any of the Bible story books in our home. I had good Sunday school teachers, but they would have been embarrassed to tell innocent children some of the stories I've come upon.

I must have had other teachers, but the ones I recall are Miss Daisy Clark, an elderly, gentle woman who seldom raised her voice above a whis-

*Postcard view of Thomasville Methodist
Church (no longer standing).*

per; Miss Julia Mary Allen, who taught me the Bible Alphabet; and Osceola Green, who sold ladies' ready-to-wear at Bedsole Dry Goods Company and was the pianist in the orchestra that played for Saturday night dances at Bradford's Pond, about fifteen miles from Thomasville. I never attended those dances though I spent many happy daytime hours at Bradford's Pond.

Strangely enough, though I cannot remember what I read in last week's *TIME*, I, after nearly eighty-five years, can still recite the entire Bible Alphabet except for the letter *Z*. I can begin with *A*, "*A* soft answer turneth away wrath," and go right through the other letters until I reach *Z*. It had something to do with Zealousness, but I don't know what.

Back to the grasshopper—Southern storytellers do tend to stray.

If I had been older, old enough to listen to and wonder about superstitions, I might really have been frightened when that insect leapt on me. There's an oft-repeated warning that if a grasshopper spits in your eye, you'll go blind. Maybe that's why Effie brushed the intruder away so quickly.

Effie never talked to me about superstitions, but later our beloved cook, Thurza, did. Thurza wore a silver dime (all dimes were pure silver back then) tied around her ankle with a cotton string to bring good luck. Or was it to ward off evil? I forget. I do know she stuck a wooden match in her hair to cure a headache.

Mother would offer Thurza an aspirin, but she always replied, "No thank you, ma'am. I just like to use matches."

I liked to use matches too, not for curing headaches (I've never had a half a dozen in my whole long life) but for the fun of striking them, the magic of making fire. The only punishment I remember receiving as a child was for striking matches. I was about four or five years old, and I had been instructed never to strike matches unless there was an adult supervising me.

One day I disobeyed, and Mother caught me in the act. "You like to strike matches, don't you?" she said. "Well, I'll let you strike all you want to."

She took me into the living room, sat me down in my little chair on the hearth, and handed me a new box of two hundred and fifty matches.

"Strike them all," she told me.

Somehow it was no longer fun to make those blue-tipped matches burst into flame. The more I struck, the less fun it became. "Can't I stop now, please?" I begged.

"No," Mother replied. She was rocking and reading the *Literary Digest*. "You like to strike matches. Keep on. The box isn't even half empty yet."

So I kept on. There was no reprieve despite my pleas and tears. By the time I struck the last match, my fascination with "making fire" had vanished forever.

There were matches in every room of our house. We needed them to light the fires in the fireplaces in cold weather, and we needed them to light candles and lamps year'round. The power to fuel our electric lighting came from the local sawmill which shut down at 10:30 every night and did not begin running again until 5:00 or 6:00 in the morning.

The night watchman at the mill blinked the lights at 10:00 and again at 10:20 every night, warning that they were about to go out. After 10:30 P.M. the whole town was dark. Dates always ended with the first blinking of the lights although sometimes the sweet farewells ran on until 10:20. For a young man to loiter at his sweetheart's house after the lights went out created a right smart of gossip in the neighborhood.

One night Eric Clark, one of my early Sunday school teacher's three grown sons, got caught in town after the lights went out. The Clark family lived on the outskirts of Thomasville, and while he was trying to make his way home in the total darkness, Eric fell in the same ditch three times. Fortunately, he was not injured.

When he did get home, he felt his way out to the sleeping porch where his brothers were already in bed, and he created quite a commotion stumbling around in the dark. One sleepy brother

*With my father, downtown
Thomasville, 1920.*

asked, "What are you doing, Eric?"

"I'm trying to find a lantern so I can light it and go back to town and see how dark it is!"

Eric was mighty happy when the Alabama Power Company came to town about 1927. Everybody was.

We had this reliable source of electricity before we had a municipal (too big a word to apply to Thomasville) water system. I was twelve years old before we had running water (a term no longer in general use) in our house. A deep well, a dug well, on our back porch supplied our water, water that was clear and cold and pure.

Thurza used to let me stand in front of her with my hands on the well rope and help her lower the empty bucket into the well and then, when it was full, pull it up, hand over hand, again. I remember how the bucket sounded when it hit the water and how heavy it was when we pulled it up and put it on the side shelf by the well. I felt very grown up when I was allowed to draw water all by myself. Now it might be termed a "rite of passage."

A few years ago when I was talking to a group of fifth grade students, I mentioned drawing water. Not a child there knew what I was talking about; they all thought I was doing artwork, drawing a picture of water. They didn't know what a dish pan was either. And as for a slop jar . . .

Occasionally wiggle-tails infested our well, and for several days we would not be able to drink the water. Thurza would throw salt in the well to kill the wiggle-tails (I'm still not sure what they were or where they came from), and for a few days she would take a big blue and white enamel cooler to a neighbor's house to get our drinking water. I don't think Pharaoh and his people were inflicted with wiggle-tails.

Thurza could walk with that cooler of water balanced on her head, never touching it and never spilling a drop. Years later, when I was married and living in Selma, our washwoman, Betty, would put my toddler in her split-oak clothes basket, put it on her head, and saunter home. Kitti delighted in those rides.

Thurza Hillery, about 1935.

When the well really needed cleaning, the well-cleaners would come, a pair of them, one a large, strong man and the other a thin, younger fellow but also strong. They wore overalls with no shirts, and they always took off their shoes and put them on the edge of the porch. Then they would rapidly draw water from the well, bucket after bucket, emptying the water into the chicken trough near the porch or throwing it like miniature waterfalls into the back yard. Sometimes there were tiny rainbows in the waterfalls they created. On hot days, they would "accidentally" pour water on me.

When the water was down to only about ankle deep, the small man would catch hold of the rope and be lowered into the well with the bucket. He retrieved whatever objects had fallen into the well since his last visit: knives, dippers, spectacles (amazingly unscathed and unbroken), cups, towels, drink bottles, books, and such. A distant cousin once dropped his false teeth in the well, but I don't believe they were ever recovered. The items were put in the bucket and pulled from the well. It was exciting to see what treasures were in each bucket. The small man scrubbed sediment and moss from the well's lining and yanked on the rope as a signal to be pulled up. The cleaning was over.

My first lecture, delivered by my father.

Spit

My first encounter with righteous indignation occurred at that well. Before I started to school, my cousin, a city boy about my age who was visiting us from Little Rock, Arkansas, leaned over and spit in our well! If I had had the strength to push him into the well to join his spit, I would have done it. When I told Thurza what my cousin had done, she told me I shouldn't hate Louis, said he didn't know better, and she gave me a talk on the subject of forgiveness and spit.

"Spit is powerful," she said, "can take off all sorts of bad luck. Like if a rabbit runs across the road in front of your car, something bad gonna happen to you 'less you take off your hat and spit in it and put it on backwards."

Daddy kept a spit hat in the car. He believed in being prepared. There were more rabbits crossing

With big brother, Wilson.

the roads in the 1920s than there are now.

I wish I could recall all the things Thurza told me about spit. I do remember she told me if your ear itches, it's a sign somebody is saying bad things about you. You can stop the bad talk by spitting on your little finger and rubbing it in your ear. The gossiper will stop talking, Thurza said, and will get a splitting headache, one that even matches would not cure. That bit of lore pleased me.

I already knew it was good luck to spit on your baited fish hook. My brother Wilson taught me that. I did not know until Thurza told me that you will have perfect eyesight if you spit on a lightning bug in flight. I tried hard to accomplish that feat, but I never did. I was near-sighted and had to begin wearing glasses when I was in grammar school.

We had to go to Selma, sixty-five miles away, to get my eyes examined and to get my glasses fitted by Dr. Samuel Kirkpatrick. He was a tall, thin man with a clipped white mustache and precise professional manners. I never heard him laugh.

Usually we went by train with a puffing steam

Mallie Jackson, at the Thomasville depot.

engine pulling the coal car, the baggage car, the white passenger cars, and the colored passenger cars along. The backs of the plush-covered seats in the passenger car could be pushed forward or backward so that families or friends could be seated facing each other. I liked to ride backwards, but some passengers said riding backwards made them sick.

At that time, there was no air conditioning in the summertime. The grime-smeared windows in the passenger car were raised for ventilation. Though there were screens at the windows, soot and cinders blew in.

Once a cinder got in my eye soon after the train left Thomasville. Mother tried to get it out but could not. The conductor tried unsuccessfully as did two or three passengers. I tried not to cry, but the cinder hurt my eye. The butcher boy gave me one of his most popular wares, a small glass lantern filled with brightly colored candy. The gift did not ease my pain.

At the train's next stop, the conductor had

the station agent send a message to the nearest station where a doctor lived, asking the doctor to meet the train when it arrived. So when the train got to Lamison, Dr. Fudge was waiting beside the tracks. He hurried aboard, rolled my eyelid back on a little stick (it could have been a match stem) and extracted the cinder. There was no charge.

That was a long time ago. Dr. Fudge has been dead for many years, but his small, white frame office still stands vacant near the railroad track in Lamison.

Dr. Kirkpatrick, my Selma eye doctor, prescribed drops to be put in my eyes and an ointment to be rubbed on my granulated eyelids each night. Mother kept the drops on the bedroom mantel where they shared space with an assortment of medications in small bottles.

Larger containers of medicines and beauty aids were clustered on the washstand in a recessed cove in the bedroom: Fletcher's Castoria, SSS Tonic, Syrup of Figs, Honey & Almond lotion, Coconut Oil shampoo and such.

Dr. Fudge entering his office in Lamison.

One night at bedtime after brushing my hair one hundred strokes (apparently she did not believe the superstition that brushing your hair at night makes you forgetful), Mother reached up on the mantel for my eye drops and squeezed a drop in each eye. Almost at once, she realized she had used the wrong medication, so she immediately put drops from the same bottle in her eyes to find out if they hurt or burned or had any effect on her vision.

My father, who had witnessed the entire procedure, blurted out the only cross words I ever heard him say to my mother. "What's wrong with you, Helen? It's not enough that I might have a blind daughter? You want me to have a blind wife, too?"

Fortunately he was burdened with neither possibility. We washed out our eyes with water from the well, and our sight was not damaged.

On one other occasion, I saw my father give Mother a look of shocked disbelief. We had guests for dinner (noon), influential businessmen or preachers or educators or politicians or such from out of town. Thurza had cooked one of her finest meals, the long dining table was bright with flowers from Mother's garden, and one of the visitors had even complimented me on my good manners.

The conversation turned to one of the major news stories of the day. A group of Arctic explorers who had been given up as dead had been found alive on floating islands of ice.

"Isn't it miraculous that those men could have survived for nearly three weeks on ice cakes!" one guest commented.

"It certainly is amazing," Mother replied in her pleasantest tone. "I wouldn't think ice cakes had enough nourishment in them to keep anybody alive."

Daddy gave Mother a look, but he didn't say anything, just buttered two more of Thurza's hot biscuits. I almost forgot my good manners.

Accounts of life in the frigid north fascinated me. I wondered what it would be like to live in a house made of ice. Our house in Thomasville was cold in the wintertime, so cold that some nights water would freeze in the pitcher on the washstand in my room. On these bitter nights I would curl up in a tight ball when I went to bed and pretend that my feet were explorers venturing out into the Arctic. Slowly and cautiously I would push my cold feet across the frozen whiteness toward their goal. Often they had to halt their advance and establish temporary camp along the way. Occasionally they would retreat to the relative warmth of the base camp. The expanse of snow-white sheets was intimidating to the brave explorers.

On those frigid nights, Mother would warm a sweater by the fire, bring it to the bed, and wrap my feet in it. What blessed comfort! She never knew that her small act of love rescued brave explorers.

One of my favorite toys was a stuffed dog, a husky named Balto, named for a real hero. Balto was the lead sled dog in a team that ran for miles in bitter cold to deliver a vaccine to an Arctic village where diphtheria had broken out. I wish I could recall the details of the story. Daddy told me about it, and he brought me the toy dog when he came home from a business trip. He always found interesting gifts (often books) to bring home.

Once he came home from Mobile with a live chameleon chained to his coat collar. As soon as he stepped off the train, a group gathered around him to watch the small lizard change color as he was shifted to one background after another. No spectator was more charmed than I was. Daddy put him on the sleeve of my red sweater and his dark skin began to take on a reddish hue. I still don't understand how the color changes. I haven't seen a chameleon in a long time.

Second birthday.

About four years old.

First vehicle.

Sixth Grade Commencement Exercises.
Miss Shaw.

ᕮᏚᎠ

1. Welcome Song _____ Class.
2. Invocation _____ Rev. Mc Crary.
3. Salutatory _____ Eloise Dexter.
4. Class Prophecy _____ Evelyn C. Lillard.
5. Class Poems. _____ Mary Nichols.
6. Class Will. _____ Gerald Sewery.
7. Class Key. _____ James C. Lanton.
8. Gifterian _____ Ruth Williams.
9. Valedictory. _____ Kathryn Tucker.
10. Address. _____ Mr. J. W. Tucker.
11. Awarding of Diplomas _____ Mr. J. C. Ellis.
12. Farewell Song _____ Class.
13. Benediction _____ Rev. J. H. Holloway.

Thomasville Elementary School, 1930.

Varmints

THERE WAS ONE OCCASION WHEN DADDY CAME from Mobile with a real surprise. He stood at the top of the train steps with a small monkey cuddled in his arms. Mother, who had walked to the train to meet him, turned quickly and began walking up the hill toward home.

If she had not retreated so hastily, had waited a moment or two longer, Mother would have learned that it wasn't a real monkey Daddy was holding; it was a hand puppet. It did look and behave mighty real. Daddy had practiced maneuvering the puppet all the way from Mobile, much to the amusement and delight of the other passengers. He got so good at handling the puppet that one man offered the monkey a banana. Daddy told that story later. Right then he had to catch up with Mother to assure her that the monkey was not live, that it was only a puppet.

He apologized for upsetting her, and she forgave him. That monkey stayed around our house for years. Even I became proficient—though my hand was too small to fit him correctly—in making guests believe I had a real monkey for a pet.

There were two other monkey stories in Thomasville, both brief.

Jackson Grocery Company, in the heart of downtown, bought a stalk of bananas from a wholesaler in Mobile. Bracey Gates, the clerk in the store, hung the stalk from a hook near the center of the store where the customers would be sure to see the bananas and could pull off the ones they wanted to buy.

One of the first customers, a good housewife, was yanking her selections from the stalk when something that she had no intention of buying fell out: it was a tiny monkey, a live monkey. Word spread quickly and lots of folks came to Jackson's Grocery to see the monkey and to buy bananas.

Business was so good that Elo Jackson had to telephone Mobile to order another stalk of bananas.

The other monkey story involved a little circus that came to town and put on a show in the lumber yard, across the road from our house. The lumber yard was a favorite place for small circuses, medicine shows, and revival meetings to pitch a tent.

My sister Annelee (I was born the night she graduated from high school, and she never forgave me for stealing the spotlight from her graduation) and her date were among the spectators around the circus ring that night. A monkey that had been riding a horse with a trick rider escaped during the act, and the trainer could not catch him.

Females shrieked all around the tent, none louder than my sister who was afraid of many things. She screamed even louder when she looked down and saw the animal crouching right beneath her seat. Her outburst frightened the monkey away, but by then Annelee was in hysterics and kept repeating, "Take me home! Take me home!" So her date did just that.

The short walk across the lumber yard and up the street to our house calmed Annelee somewhat, but the calm was short-lived. When they got home, the monkey was sitting on the top step waiting to greet her.

Enough about monkeys.

As I recall, I was a patient at the Baptist Hospital in Selma when Daddy brought me one of my best-loved gifts, a toy Victrola. I was a puny child and was a patient at that hospital rather often. I have a few clear memories of those hospital stays. One memory is of the constant, or so it seemed, diet of gummy oatmeal. I had to eat so much of it there when I was very young that I never ate another bit of it until I was in my seventies.

Another memory is of how thirsty I was after my adenoids and tonsils were removed. I must have been six or seven years old. When I "came to" from the ether-induced sleep, my one request was for water. The nurse kept telling me that they had sent to town for some ice, and as soon as the ice arrived, I could have water. It was a long miserable wait.

A happier memory is of being wrapped in a blanket and carried in my nurse's arms (I called her "Miss Buzzard") across a vacant field to the bank of the Alabama River to watch a steamboat go by. I was too young to realize that I was watching the end of an era of river transportation. We waved at the boat as it passed and an officer blew the boat's deep whistle in reply.

I was older when Aunt Bet talked to me about her childhood memories of steamboats. Her father, Edward Tabb, the grandfather I never knew, was in charge of the warehouse and commissary at Tuskahoma, a major steamboat landing on the Tombigbee River.

Aunt Bet liked to describe the luxurious furnishings in the ladies' parlors and the fine food served on the linen-covered tables in the mess hall. Maybe she called them dining rooms. Her real joy, however, was describing the sounds of the boat-whistles. Each boat had a distinctive whistle, and as a child, she recognized each one. Sometimes she tried to imitate the different sounds for me, and we would

Being held by Aunt Bet, left; and by my mother.

both laugh. Our laughter never lessened her longing for the golden days of river transportation nor her wish to hear the whistles of steamboats again. My mother, Helen Tabb, was born at Tuskahoma, a landmark that is no longer shown on maps.

As I said, it was during one of those hospital stays that Daddy brought me the toy Victrola. It was a music box encased in a miniature wooden replica of a real music machine. It stood about eight inches high on its stubby legs, had slanted sides and a top that let up and down. When the key on the side was wound and the top let down, it played "Oh, You Beautiful Doll."

I loved that little Victrola and played it until its music box wore completely out. The silent shell is still here on a closet shelf somewhere.

The first real Victrola I ever heard was in Mr. Vance Nored's store. It was taller than I was and had a crank on the side to wind it up. Some adults told me there were real little men playing the guitar and singing inside. I hope I didn't believe them.

I was a little older when Wilson brought a record

With Wilson, about 1921.

player home and taught me to dance. I stood on his feet as he danced me around the living room to the tune of "My Blue Heaven." Wilson was a graceful dancer.

He also excelled at baseball, football, basketball, fishing, and hunting. He was too skinny to be a lineman on the football team, but he was an elusive runner and an effective tackler in the backfield. He played on the offensive team and on the defensive team in every game. All players did then. My mother never went to the football games. She used to say she didn't know whether it was harder to stay at home and worry about Wilson's getting hurt in the game or to be present and see him injured, so she stayed at home and prayed.

Daddy attended the games, and he was a knowledgeable critic of the action on the field. If he decided Wilson was playing sloppily, wasn't doing his best, Daddy would step to the edge of the field (most observers walked up and down the sidelines following the action of the game), motion to Wilson to run over to him, and send

Wilson home. There was never any consultation with the coach (one coach did it all back then), and Wilson never hesitated about leaving the game and walking home.

By the time I was old enough to be a cheerleader in high school, Wilson, who studied engineering at Auburn, was working for the Missouri Highway Department building bridges. I missed him and used to beg him to come back home. He would tell me, "I'll come back to Alabama when those bridges I built north of Thomasville shake." They still don't shake.

About cheerleading: I watch the young women today on television and sometimes in person, and I marvel at how little they wear and how expertly they perform athletic feats. Some of them could win gold medals in the Olympics. My cheerleading outfit consisted of long white pants, a white turtleneck sweater with big red letters THS sewed on the front, and a blue and crimson cape made by Miss Mellie McCurdy. Not an inch of flesh showed.

We didn't build pyramids or do flips. We didn't

even jump very high. We did lead the faithful in cheers (yells) and songs such as

> O, Thomasville had a tiger
> With long and grizzly hair,
> And Grove Hill had a bulldog,
> Now wouldn't they make a pair!
> And when they get together
> There's sure to be a scrap.
> Just watch that Thomasville tiger
> Wipe that bulldog off the map.

We were also good at leading chants such as, "Hold that line. Hold that line," and "Touchdown, Thomasville! Touchdown, Thomasville!"

It was all so discreet and so long ago.

Actually, we didn't need cheerleaders if Mr. Walter Ingram, who lived in the nearby community of Bashi, attended the game. He had the loudest, most penetrating voice I've ever heard, and he would run up and down the sidelines shouting encouragement and instructions to the team. Fans in neighboring

*In my Thomasville High cheerleader
uniform, 1934.*

towns used to offer to pay Mr. Ingram to come holler for their team, but he remained faithful to Thomasville.

Wilson sent me two presents from Missouri: a Scotch Collie puppy that I named Sikes (Wilson was living in Sikeston at the time) and a huge owl. Both arrived several years apart, by railroad in slatted wooden crates addressed to me.

Sikes was a wished-for, welcome gift, but the owl presented problems. He was an impressive bird, but my family and I were unprepared to take care of the hooter. We released him into my playhouse in the back yard. The space was adequate, and the wire screening on the sides made it like a large cage, but feeding and watering the bird was difficult.

After my playmates and a good many neighbors had come to admire the owl, we let him go. I left the door of my playhouse open and stood on the porch near the well and watched as he flew to freedom, sailing above our peach orchard and heading to the woods in Hill's Pasture.

That owl was the only gift Wilson ever gave me

*Beryl Coleman, Evelyn Cleiland, and Huey Ford
in the log cabin we built ourselves in Hill's pasture.*

that I did not like. I proudly wore the orange and blue "rat cap" he got me as a freshman at Alabama Polytechnic Institute (Auburn), and, though they did not survive, I loved the live baby squirrels and rabbits he brought me from his hunts. When he was still in grammar school, before he was old enough to wear long pants (this was many years ago), Wilson was said to be the most accurate shot in the area. In his earliest letter to Santa Claus, his only request was for a box of shells.

He taught me how to shoot an air rifle as soon as I was big enough to hold a gun, showed me how to keep the gun steady, aim down the barrel and squeeze the trigger. We would line up tin cans (Prince Albert tobacco cans were prize targets) on our back fence, and I would shoot.

One afternoon when I was about six years old, Wilson took me hunting with him. We rode his bicycle to the nearest woods. I sat side-saddle style on the metal bar connecting the seat and the handlebars, and I held Wilson's gun. In Thomasville we called it "double-heading" when two people rode a bicycle together. As soon as we entered the woods, Wilson told me, "Spit on the barrel of the gun. It will bring us good luck." I did and it did.

We had not taken six steps before Wilson saw and shot a squirrel. "Go get him, Katink," he said. By the time I returned, carrying the dead squirrel by his bushy tail the way Wilson had taught me, Wilson was seated on a knoll with his back to a tree. He never got up all afternoon, just slid slowly around the tree as he spotted squirrels and shot them. "Go get him," he would tell me each time he pulled the trigger. He never missed. I must have trotted fifty miles that afternoon retrieving Wilson's trophies. Our family had a good supper of squirrel stew and fried squirrel that night, but I was too tired to eat.

One time Wilson brought a young possum home inside his hunting coat. I couldn't imagine having a possum for a pet; the creature was so ugly! Mother told Wilson he could keep the possum but he had to promise to confine the marsupial to his room. Wilson promised.

I'm sure he meant to keep his word, but somehow that animal escaped into the recesses of our rambling house. We searched everywhere for him to no avail. My sister Annelee, at home on vacation from teaching school, was terrorized, as usual, and she even offered a reward of one dollar to anyone who found the possum.

I searched diligently for a day or two, but my incentive dwindled when Annelee offered to pay me twenty-five cents a night to sleep with her as protection from a possible prowling possum. Thinking back, I know that the role of possum protector was an unlikely, even absurd, role for a little girl, but it was the most and easiest money I'd ever had. I was mighty disappointed when Thurza found the varmint hanging by his tail behind a curtain in the living room.

Wilson, following Mother's orders, captured the possum and immediately returned him to his native habitat. He likely shot a squirrel or two on the way home.

Something else about possums: they are immune to snake bites and they continue to grow all their lives. True!

Although Wilson's skill with a gun was talked about and envied, it was his marksmanship with a much simpler weapon that earned him fame.

When he was in high school, it was his job to sweep out the bank, empty the waste baskets, and so forth before the bank opened each day. For weeks the employees had complained about the damage done each night by a big wood rat that nested in the building. They put out poison and they set strong traps, but the rat escaped death and continued his nightly rampages. The creature even became bold enough to run through the lobby in the daytime now and then.

One morning when Wilson was cleaning up, he saw the rat looking at him, taunting him, Wilson said, from a hole in the baseboard. Wilson picked up a rubber band and a paper clip off the desk, shot the rat in the eye and killed him. It was Wilson's most famous feat of marksmanship ever, was talked about for years.

There is another rat story in our family, not a pretty story. Just before I married, back in 1946, the interior of our house in Thomasville was painted. Mother was living with Aunt Bet and Tabb, and I was working for the *Birmingham News*. The house was all spruced up for the big event.

Then, a few days before the wedding, a large wood rat got in the house, a rat possibly kin to the one Wilson had killed years earlier. The intruder was chased into the dining room where the refreshments were to be served and where the Nicola Marshall portrait of Uncle Doc Underwood looked down on the proceedings. The pursuers, armed with broom and fire pokers, cast many blows at their victim, but he escaped each blow.

Things got worse. As the rat scurried across the room seeking an escape, someone stepped on his tail. "Got him now!" she exclaimed.

How wrong she was! The rat yanked away from the foot, leaving only the skin from his tail. Then, waving his bloody appendage, he continued to run and jump all around the room until he was finally

Aunt Bet with my wedding cake,
with Uncle Doc Underwood looking on.

dispatched by someone wielding a poker.

The rat was dead, but the room was a bloody mess. Painters had to return to cover the blood-stained walls and floor. The dining room looked lovely for the reception. No mention was made of the rat. Even Uncle Doc Underwood appeared to be pleased—and very relieved.

One more Wilson story.

When Wilson was in high school, the principal was a well-educated, smart man, but he had no notion about how to maintain discipline. Students, especially the older boys, took full advantage of his ignorance.

The school building was frame, two stories tall with the grammar school on the first floor and the high school on the second. It stood in a grove of oak trees which were favorite feeding stations for local squirrels.

So Wilson and his friends—Cousin Earl, Russell Stutts and others—took their guns to school with them. They chose desks at the windows of their classrooms and propped their weapons against the wall. When the squirrels became active, the boys ignored their school work and, still seated at their desks, shot out through the open windows, always killing squirrels.

In this day of metal detectors, when possession of even a small pocket knife is ground for expulsion, I wonder how the authorities would deal with squirrel hunting in school. My father, when he learned of it, administered his own brand of discipline, and he confiscated Wilson's gun. That was the worst punishment of all.

Daddy would likely not have learned of the guns at school, at least not as soon as he did, if those teenagers had not pulled an outrageously dangerous prank on the principal. Since Thomasville did not have a water system (running water) there were, of course, no inside toilets at school. The facilities were housed in two long buildings, one for boys and one for girls, on the edge of the campus. Two private one-seaters nearby served the needs of the faculty.

One day at recess, Wilson and his cohorts saw

the principal enter the private privy. They rushed to the scene, leaned against the door and set the building on fire. When the principal saw the smoke, he pled with his captors to release him, calling those boys by grown-up names: "Mr. Tucker, please let me out! Mr. Stutts, I can't breathe—please don't let me die in here. Please let me out!" They opened the door and the captive escaped physically unharmed.

Those school boys should have been sent to jail, but they weren't.

The principal left town, and a very strict disciplinarian took his place.

*My father, J. W. Tucker,
at the bank's side door.*

Lightning

A FEW YEARS LATER, DURING WILSON'S DAYS AT Auburn, he and one of his friends were badly in need of money, so they went into the lightning-rod-charging business, a successful if short-lived enterprise. There aren't lightning rods on many rural houses now (they've become an endangered species along with dug wells and outhouses and dial telephones) but they used to be fairly common.

Wilson and his buddy would drive out in the country and stop at a house with a lightning rod. They would introduce themselves as engineering students from Alabama Polytechnic Institute who were doing a survey of lightning rods. That was mostly true. Then they would ask questions about the make of the lightning rod and how long the protective device had been in place. They listened intently to the answers, and made notes in the tablets they carried. They also discussed the various aspects of the apparatus, using technical terms between themselves.

Then came the critical question: how long since the lightning rod had been charged?

The young engineers were always shocked to learn that the lightning rod had never been charged. Never. They then explained the potential danger of uncharged rods to the property owner and his family. While the man was recovering from the shock of learning how ineffective uncharged rods could be, how hazardous living in an unprotected house could be, the conniving pair offered to rectify the situation by charging the rod for just one dollar.

Wilson stuttered badly, so his companion did most of the talking. Wilson handled the engineering part. He took a long piece of copper wire out of the back seat of the Model A Ford, and raised the hood. He hooked one end of the wire to the lightning rod and the other end to the engine of the car, revved the engine and let it run for a minute or two, counting the seconds aloud. His cohort explained that the charging time was related to the height of the lightning rod and to its compass location. The procedure required precision.

Then when it was safe to unhook the copper wire, the pair collected their dollar, accepted the thanks of the donor and went in search of the next victim.

Business was good until one of their customers came in the bank one day and said to Daddy, "You've got a fine son. I'd never met him until he came by the house yesterday and charged my lightning rod for me."

When Daddy learned the whole story, he made the budding entrepreneurs return all their earnings.

I still look for lightning rods when I ride out in the country, look for the simple ones and the fancy ones with ornate metal decorations and bright glass balls. I have one such protector out in my storage shed somewhere. I've intended for years to have it installed on my roof. However, it wouldn't do much good; it never has been charged.

Years ago an older colored man told me he had several lightning bolts. They were heavy pieces of iron shaped like Zs, he said. During a summer storm he watched as a bolt of lightning struck a tree in his yard, peeling off the bark and burying itself in the ground. He went out after the weather cleared, he said, and dug up several bolts of lightning from around the roots of that tree. He promised to bring me one, but he never did.

He knew, of course, that it is bad luck to burn the wood from a tree that has been struck by lightning. Everybody knows that. He also knew that if you sit in the middle of a feather bed during a storm, lightning won't strike you. Thurza taught me that.

I've never been sure whether it was true or was merely a superstition that the telephone receivers should be taken off the hooks and allowed to dangle down during a thunderstorm. This was back in the days of wall telephones with a crank on one side to ring up Central and a receiver with a brown cord on a hook on the other side.

As a child, it was my duty to take the receiver off the hook, to bring in the cretonne-covered cushions from the front porch, and to turn the porch rocking chairs around and lean them against the wall when a thunderstorm approached.

Wall telephones have virtually disappeared now, as have such materials as cretonne, pongee, dotted Swiss (my dotted Swiss Easter dress always scratched), and flour sacking. Also gone are skate keys, real rubber hot water bottles, wire egg beaters, coal scuttles, ice picks, and plain fire pokers.

As a child, the main pleasure of having a fire in the fireplace was poking the burning wood or coal and scraping down plumes of soot from the back and sides of the fireplace.

"You know what happens to children who play in the fire," adults often warned me. I knew. I'd heard it often enough. "If you play in the fire you will wet the bed." I knew, but I was willing to run the risk. I still am. Gas logs are practical and sometimes attractive, but they are no fun. You can't toast marshmallows in the flames, and, because

Not dotted swiss,
but soft, accordion-pleated material.

there are no ashes, you can't roast eggs (wrapped in wet newspapers) or sweet potatoes. And it was so satisfying to scrape the sides and back of a real fireplace with a poker.

Other scrapings were fun: scraping or licking the dasher of the ice cream freezer. Few children today know the pure pleasure of helping to make homemade ice cream, chipping the ice, filling the freezer, turning the crank, adding coarse ice cream salt, and finally licking the dasher. I used to sit on a folded towel on top of the freezer to hold it steady when the custard began to harden and the handle became difficult to turn.

As I grow older, I miss so many simple things. Do children play anymore? I seldom see them outside except at organized sporting events. It has been a long time since I saw hop-scotch squares drawn on a sidewalk or heard a child call out, "Bushel of wheat, bushel of rye. All ain't hid holler out I!" followed by "Bushel of wheat, bushel of clover. All ain't hid can't hide over!" And I wonder if anybody shoots marbles anymore. Do children know what

Playing with my nephew Billy Ryan in the lumberyard.

*Playing at the lumberyard. Parents today
would have a stroke.*

Hard Down Knucks means? Do they play Tag, or Hide the Switch, or May I? or Chinese Rock School or Red Light? Games of Drop the Handkerchief and even Pin the Tail on the Donkey have virtually disappeared from the birthday party scene.

Has any child you know ever fished for a doodle bug? Such a simple pastime. Bessie Gray taught me how to spit on a broom straw, dip the damp end in dust, and poke it down a doodle bug's hole.

The chant that accompanied this fishing expedition began, "Doodle bug, doodle bug, your house is on fire. Your children are burning up—" I can't recall the rest of it. Sometimes Bessie Gray and I caught doodle bugs on our spit-baited straws. Sometimes we didn't. But it was fun.

Playing with June bugs was fun, too. They were easy to catch, especially in fig season. Tying a thread around the prickly hind leg of the green beetle was the hard part, but Bessie Gray could do it skillfully. She also knew how long the thread needed to be to allow our captives to zoom in circles around our heads to entertain us and to tether the green "airplanes" to a tree branch when we went in search of other diversions.

And where have all the paper dolls gone? My playmates Beryl and Johnnie Lou and Waverly and I used to spend hours cutting out paper dolls from the fashion sections of *The Delineator* or *Pictorial Review*. We had whole families of paper dolls—father, mother, babies, little children, teenagers, even grandparents—who were filed by age (there were often long arguments whether a cut-out belonged in the fourteen or fifteen age group) between the pages of a discarded magazine. Each paper doll had clothes for any occasion filed neatly away, and if their countenance changed with each costume change, it didn't disturb us at all.

Scarey Ann

DOLLS WERE DIFFERENT. THEY BECAME SOME-
what worn and their complexions faded, but their
faces remained the same. Roanoke Jane was one
of my favorites. She was a big cloth doll made in
Roanoke, Alabama, by some process that made the
doll's face, arms, and feet hard. There was Mibbs
whose face peeled so badly that she had to be sent
to a doll hospital in another state for treatment.
I missed her. Scarey Ann was a painted wooden
doll with a button in her back. When you pushed
that button, Scarey Ann's stiff black hair stood
on end.

I had not thought of Scarey Ann (she had a
green dress painted on her wooden body) in years
until I began writing about my dolls. I inquired
of my older friends about their dolls, and I was
surprised that none of them had ever even heard

of Scarey Ann. Then I asked doll dealers about her, and they also confessed their ignorance. One or two friends tried to find her on the Internet or computer or such, but their searches were not successful.

I was about to think I had created the doll in my imagination, that such a toy never existed. It was a disconcerting, bordering on being frightening, feeling.

Then a persistent young woman used her electronic skills and found photographs of Scarey Ann and other dolls like her, all wooden and all hand-painted. The inventor was a Chinese dentist in California. The dolls were created during the 1920s, exactly the right time frame for my Scarey Ann. The information and verification were vastly relieving to me. I do wish I knew how my Scarey Ann got to Thomasville, Alabama.

The one doll that did change had two screw-on heads. One head had curly hair and sweet expression like a girl. The other head was definitely masculine. Beheading a doll to change sex seemed strange even to a child like me.

SCAREY ANN

I do not have a photo of my own Scarey Ann, but it was similar to the one in this photo, which came from the Internet site of an enthusiast who collects them. The site even includes a copy of the patent drawings which show how the "hair-raising" mechanism worked.

There were other dolls, I'm sure, new dolls for birthdays and Christmas, but those are the ones I remember. The dolls Santa Claus brought always had smut on their faces, a blemish from coming down the chimney.

When we had a dime or a quarter, we bought celluloid dolls at Bedsole's Five and Ten Cent Store. The dolls were small, none taller than about six or eight inches, had movable arms and legs, and were naked.

We got scraps of cloth from whatever Mother happened to be sewing at the time, and made clothes for the dolls. That is, my playmates did. I couldn't sew. Still can't. My nude toy had to be wrapped in swaddling clothes until Bessie Gray, Thurza's teenage daughter and my close friend, could make her some clothes. Then she was the best-dressed doll in town.

Bessie Gray could look at clothes my paper dolls were wearing or study the latest fashions on models in the show window at Bedsole's Dry Goods Company and copy them exactly. Her talent amazed even the adults. She was a wonderfully imaginative, creative playmate.

She and I used to make what we called sweat bees in the backyard in the summertime. We'd dig a bowl-shaped hole about a foot in diameter and line it with green moss. Then we'd stick the stems of roses, daisies, cosmos or whatever was blooming into the moss and cover our creation with a piece of glass, usually a broken window pane that we had washed clean at the chicken trough, and seal the edges with more green moss. Our sweat bees would stay fresh for days.

We used that same kind of green moss for carpets in the playhouses we built between the roots of trees. The above-ground roots separated the rooms of the house, and Bessie Gray would furnish and decorate each room. Broken glass, acorn cups, penny match boxes, pieces of cardboard became parts of a child's playhouse world in her magical hands.

The day I turned thirteen, Bessie Gray said to me, "I can't call you Kathryn no more. I got to call you Miss Kathryn now."

"No!" I replied. "Why can't you call me Kathryn?"

"You ain't no little girl now. You a young lady. Mama say I got to call you Miss Kathryn."

And she did. After that, we were no longer playmates. I wonder what happened to Bessie Gray. Years ago she was a maid at the old Battle House Hotel in Mobile. With a little education, a little guidance, a little difference in skin color, she could have become a fashion designer. I think of her and am grateful that she taught me that simple things have beauty. I wish I could recall the songs and dances she taught me, songs such as

> John, John the barber,
> He went to shave his father.
> The razor slip
> And cut his lip.
> O, John, John the barber.

I wish I knew what that song meant. I have forgotten so many things.

AGE OF INNOCENCE

About the money to buy the celluloid dolls that Bessie Gray dressed: If I asked Mother if I could buy something, her reply was always, "Look under the candlestick."

On the mantel above the fireplace in my parents' bedroom were a large clock that needed winding every night, a cluster of bottles of assorted medications, a papier mâché bucket with childhood scenes painted on it (it was called the Little Bucket and held such things as pencil stubs, shoe buttoners, string, crochet needles, scissors, keys to nobody knew what, even recipes), and a brass candlestick. When my parents had spare change, they put it under the candlestick to be used for such luxuries as buying a length of plow line to use as a jumping rope, a watermelon, another celluloid doll, an Eskimo pie from People's Drug Company. I was so fond of Eskimo pies that I was called Eskimo Pie. The nickname was later shortened to Pie. Now, when I go to Thomasville, there's nobody left to call me Pie except Boolie Cogle, who is my age and never outgrew his nickname.

Boolie and I were born in 1918, so we were the right age in 1930 when Eastman Kodak Company gave a free Brownie Kodak to thousands of twelve-year-olds all across the country. On give-away day, I got up before daylight and went to sit on the edge of the high sidewalk at People's Drug Company, the official Kodak dealer in Thomasville so I could get my Brownie before their supply ran out. Boolie was in the line behind me.

I don't know what pictures Boolie took with his Brownie, but at least two of the ones I took at age twelve have been exhibited at art museums. One, "Woman with Spinning Wheel," is the best picture I've ever taken.

My father, that summer day I took the picture, had asked if I'd like to ride with him on a business trip to Marengo County. I was eager to go. "Don't forget to bring your Brownie," he reminded me. I needed no reminder.

We stopped at a farm house in rural Marengo County, and Daddy said, "I want you to see the spinning wheel that belonged to your grandmother."

*"Woman with Spinning Wheel," taken
with my Brownie Kodak, 1930.*

With Daddy's help, the present owner of the spinning wheel brought it out to a sunny spot on the porch. She was a pleasant woman, elderly but not old, and she touched that old wheel with dignity and pride. I took one photograph. Back then taking multiple images quickly was impossible; you either got a good photograph or you didn't. There were no second chances, and you had to wait a few days before the negative was developed and printed.

The photograph I took that day with my Brownie Kodak was perfect: the lighting, the composition, even the expression on the woman's face were all exactly right. It is discouraging, even humiliating, to admit that even with modern photographic equipment and years of experience I'm not as good a photographer as I was with my first camera at age twelve.

Woman With Rooster   Kathryn Tucker Windham

"Woman with Rooster," taken half a century later.

Roosters and Tom Walkers

THE ONLY RIVAL TO THE SPINNING WHEEL PHOtograph was one I took some fifty years later, a picture I call "Woman with Rooster."

I was driving in Marengo County, going down one of Governor Big Jim Folsom's farm-to-market roads, when I saw a woman walking toward me. She was carrying a rooster in her arms. Something about the colorful plumage of the rooster, the prideful way the woman cradled it, and the woman's dignified bearing made me stop my car and ask if I might take a photograph. She nodded in agreement. I'm glad I stopped.

That rooster reminded me of a foul fowl my father gave me once. As I wrote earlier, I was a somewhat sickly child. At times my appetite deserted me, and the whole family would encourage me to eat. Whether my failure to eat was due to sickness or stubbornness, I'm not sure. One day mother asked what I would like to eat, and I told her I'd like fried chicken. My request was challenging. It was not the right season for fried chicken. Big chicken houses and processing plants did not exist in Thomasville and environs, so our small grocery store (they were not affiliated with chains) had frying-size chickens only in certain parts of the year.

Daddy, not easily discouraged, sent out word that I wanted fried chicken, and a farmer out near Bashi brought a live, frying-size rooster to give him. Daddy hurried up the hill to our house to show me the rooster before Thurza wrung his neck and fried him.

He put the rooster on my bed. "Here's your fried chicken," he laughed.

I did not laugh. The rooster looked at me and I looked at him, and all desire for fried chicken vanished. "Don't kill him! I want to play with him."

So the rooster was released unharmed in our backyard where he established his supremacy while I recuperated.

As soon as I was well enough, I went out in the backyard, called (Thurza taught me the proper sounds), and he came running. So did all the other chickens. I shooed the uninvited poultry away, and my new pet ate chicken feed from my hand. I was delighted. This happy arrangement lasted three or four weeks.

Then one day after I had fed him and was returning to the house, he followed me and pecked my heels. I was surprised and a little frightened. My pet was a big grown rooster, no longer frying size. In a few days, he became more aggressive. After eating from my hand, he would chase me to the house, pecking my heels as I ran. No matter how fast I ran, he would catch me, and his hard, sharp beak made my heels bleed.

One afternoon Daddy happened to witness the drama. Two days later we had chicken pie for dinner. Thurza made the best chicken pie in the world, but I didn't eat any.

During Mr. Rooster's reign in our backyard, I was deprived of some of my favorite activities.

With my nephews, Jimmy and Billy Ryan,
as they ride a pony (not mine).

I didn't dare play on my acting bar. Nearly every child had an acting bar, a sawed-off broom stick hung by a rope from a sturdy tree limb. My acting bar was hung from a big chinaberry tree limb. A chinaberry tree in the yard is supposed to bring good luck, but they are now about as scarce as acting bars. You could skin the cat (remember?) on an acting bar or you could hang by your knees with your head almost touching the ground as you swayed gently back and forth.

If I had hung by my knees, Mr. Rooster might have come and pecked my face and head. He could have pecked my eyes out!

His presence also robbed me of the fun of walking on Tom walkers. Some people called them stilts. I could step from the back porch on to my Tom walkers and amble all around the yard, but my heels would still be in range for rooster pecks.

After I was grown, I tried to find out why they were called Tom walkers. I got all sorts of answers, none of which made sense to me. One learned professor told me the Devil was often referred to as Old Tom. He had cloven feet, my instructor said, and since stilts (his word) often had deep notches cut on their bottoms to keep them from slipping, they resembled the Devil's footprints, so they bore his name. That explanation was too complicated, even too illogical. It took me years to find out that the name came from peeping Toms who used them to be tall enough to peep in ladies' windows. The Tom part came from the man who peeped at Lady Godiva when she rode naked down the streets in London. That made sense.

I had to forgo, temporarily, two other childhood pleasures because of the rooster's attacks: making mud pies and building frog houses.

Using damp dirt near the well, Bessie Gray and I created beautifully decorated mud pies. If we made them early enough in the morning, the sun would bake them perfectly by the time Daddy came home at noon for dinner. I always gave the most spectacular mud pie to him. He would accept it graciously, admire its decorations and save it for his dessert. Not many adults appreciated my mud pies the way Daddy did, so not many adults were accorded the honor of receiving them. Roanoke Jane, Mibbs, Scarey Ann, and even Balto welcomed them at tea parties.

Frog houses were fun to make. It was summertime fun because only bare feet could mold a proper frog house. Here's how to build a frog house: pack damp sand or dirt firmly over the top and around the sides of a bare foot, then slowly ease the foot out of what then resembles an igloo but what we knew as a frog house.

Sometimes Bessie Gray and I built whole villages, landscaped villages, of frog houses with trees and flower gardens and even petalled paths.

We also had the only lighted frog houses I ever heard of. I do not think I was a cruel child, but I would pinch off the luminous tails of lightning bugs and press them into the ceilings of our frog houses. Thurza assured us that frogs really did spend the night in our houses. And, of course, she warned us never to touch a frog lest we get warts.

I wish I had heeded her advice. When I was a

little older, my friend Ruth and I put a frog in our teacher's desk drawer during recess. I don't know where we got the frog but we had it, the room was empty, and the temptation was great. We yielded. The teacher entered the room, sat at her desk, opened the drawer to get her lesson plans, and the frog hopped out into her lap. At first she was startled, but then she was livid with anger.

"Who did this?" she demanded. She had blazing dark eyes.

I was about to confess when my boyfriend, Lyles Carter, looked at me, shook his head and said, "I did it, Miss Pearce."

Miss Pearce was not surprised. Lyles Carter was often in trouble, paid many visits to the principal's office. On this occasion, I heard the licks, licks that should have been applied to me.

As he returned, he turned to me, smiled and mouthed, "It's OK." Later when I tried to thank him he shrugged it off. "It's nothing," he said. "That's the third whipping I've had this week."

Lyles Carter and I remained close friends all

Lyles Carter Walker, friend and boyfriend, 1934.

through school though sometimes he had other girl friends and I went with other boys. When our senior class, the class of 1935, went on its outing to Bradford's Pond (even a trip to the Alabama coast was out of the question those Depression years) he and I were together all day. His dives off the high tower were as graceful as any dive I've ever seen, even in the Olympics. He could also play the piano, though few people knew of that talent. He was in high school when he decided to take piano lessons. He wanted to learn to play "The Scarf Dance," and he did. He stopped his piano lessons when he achieved that goal.

That day at Bradford's Pond, after the exhibition of his diving skills, he and I stayed out in a rowboat all day. Lyles Carter wove a crown of water lilies for me to wear. It was a magical day.

The magic vanished when he rowed us back to join our classmates for late afternoon refreshments. I was sunburned, not just plain sunburned but cooked. By the time I got home I was miserable. I spent two days in bed, covered with calamine lo-

With Ruth Williams and Tom Hadley Tyson (not a class member) on the Thomasville High senior trip to Beck's Landing on the Alabama River, 1935.

Clowning in a jalopy with Ruth Williams, 1933.

tion and every other remedy suggested for relieving sunburn. Even the thought of putting on clothes was painful.

Only one or two members of that graduating class are still alive, but they all left stories, all sorts of stories, behind. Two of my friends were the only boys I'd ever known who ran away from home. The duo, one of them the son of the Baptist preacher, were members of the high school band, and both were good musicians.

During our band's annual trip to Mobile to play in the Mardi Gras parades, they met members of the Boys Industrial School band and were impressed by their musical skills and by the band director who taught them. A day or so after our band returned home from Mardi Gras, the two boys disappeared. They did not report to school nor did anybody see them all day long. Supper time came. No boys.

A search party was organized, but the members did not know where to search. Somebody suggested setting the bloodhounds on their trail, but before those plans could be put into action, the engineer on a freight train reported seeing two boys walking along the tracks near Kimbrough. The lost were soon found.

They were amazed to learn that the Boys Industrial School was really just a nice name for the reform school. For years they were teased about being so dumb they ran away from home to enroll in a reform school.

*After high school, I entered
Montgomery's Huntingdon College.*

Admiring Aunt Bet's prize azaleas during a
spring holiday visit back to Thomasville.

Running Away

I RAN AWAY FROM HOME ONCE. I WAS FOUR OR FIVE years old, and I have long forgotten what injustice prompted me to bid my family farewell. I had gone down our long front steps and was almost to the sidewalk when Mother asked, "Where are you going?"

"I'm going to be Mr. Alex Hall's little girl," I replied.

I could hardly have chosen a more inappropriate haven. Mr. Alex Hall was an old, crippled, crotchety man who had a small shoe repair shop across the street from the Methodist Church. He lived with his old, unmarried sisters, twins, but neither crippled nor crotchety. His shoe repair business was housed in a weathered, very small, one-room building. The door had a hasp latch with

GEORGE WASHINGTON

With Jimmie Wills as Martha, in 1922, probably about the same time as I decided to run away.

a big padlock on it, and an open fireplace took up the other end of the building. There was a small shuttered window on each wall. His cluttered shop smelled of leather and shoe polish and ashes and mold and age.

Mr. Alex Hall (he was always called by all three words) was a slight man, had a withered leg that swayed back and forth when he walked on his crutches, and his round head with its fringe of white hair seemed too big for his body. I never really saw his eyes; they were squeenched behind the smudged oval glasses he wore.

Why I decided to be his little girl I'll never know. We had never had a conversation. Two or three times Mother had sent me to take a piece of pie or a slice of cake to him while she stood on the corner to watch me safely across the street. Perhaps I felt sorry for him. I don't know. I do know that I changed my mind and returned home before I got to the corner.

It was years later when my youngest daughter decided to leave home. She was about the same age I was when I set out to be Mr. Alex Hall's little girl. I don't recall the issue involved in her departure either, but it was obviously serious, too hurtful to be talked about. She got out her little suitcase, a gift from her grandmother, and packed it with what she deemed necessities. By the time she finished packing, darkness had fallen.

Her preparations completed, she trudged to the front door, flung it open and proclaimed, "I'm going out into the dark and let the mad dogs bite me!"

Just as I had done years earlier, she came back home when she reached the corner of the block. Her mission had failed, but she had added a new saying to our family collection. Now when the world is too much with us, when problems or disappointments surround us, we are likely to say, "I'm going out into the dark and let the mad dogs bite me!" Those words help put upsetting happenings into perspective.

My mother added several words and phrases to our family's collection of sayings. Serigamy is a made-up word her family used for generations to

My family provided a lifetime store of sayings and stories. From left, Bill Ryan, Edith Tucker Ryan, Aunt Bet Forster, Tabb Forster, Helen Tabb Tucker, Jimmy Ryan, and Annelee Tucker, 1930s.

*Homecoming dinner on the grounds
at Bethel Church, 1930s.*

describe a whole lot of, a good many, a heap of. It is a satisfying roll-off-the-tongue word. She never used profanity (horrors!) or even slang. If something displeased her or went awry, she dismissed it with, "O, toototerly!" Whatever pleased her or was just right was "the very dinktum!"

If I complained about food being too hot, her response was, "Heat will cool if greed will wait." I repeated those words to my children, and they passed them along. Once when my kindergarten-age grandson was visiting me, I asked him to bless our food at a meal. He said, "God is good. God is great. Heat will cool if greed will wait." Mother would have laughed at that.

Her reply when I said I did not get anything from a sermon or a recital or a lecture on a book was, "Diving and finding no pearls in the sea, blame not the ocean. The fault is with thee." I repeat those lines to myself often.

The worst thing Mother ever said about anybody was, "I do not admire him." Other people's descriptions of sorry, disreputable, really bad people faded into nothingness compared with Mother's calm, straight-lipped pronouncement of "I do not admire him."

One of the people she did not especially admire (he was a borderline case) was my Uncle Bertie who was very rich and very stingy and owned a drug store in Grove Hill. He was my deceased father's brother. When Uncle Bertie died, I drove down from Selma to Thomasville to take Mother to the funeral.

(I've never understood why she, one of the most independent women I've ever known, never learned to drive. Now my own children and grandchildren do not understand why I have never learned to use a computer or a fax, have never sent or received e-mail and do not own a cell phone.)

I arrived long before funeral time, but Mother wanted to go to Grove Hill right away. I kept insisting that we should wait awhile before making the twelve-mile drive, but she kept insisting that we leave at once.

Finally I asked, "Why are you in such a hurry

to go to Uncle Bertie's funeral, Mother?" Her reply
was, "I can't wait to hear what the preacher has
thought up to say good about Bertie."

What the preacher thought up to say about
Bertie was, "He could drive a straight nail." That
comment fits in well with my son's assessment of
his baby sister's behavior at her christening. She
screamed and yelled so loudly that nobody in the
congregation heard a word the minister said.

As soon as we walked out of the church, the baby
was quiet and smiling and sweet. Her four-year-old
brother who adored her, said in her defense, "Well,
at least she didn't spit up!"

Thus another phrase was added to our family
sayings.

Mother excelled at many things, but house-
keeping ranked low on her list of interests. She
liked to read and was instrumental in establishing
Thomasville's first public library. She was a char-
ter member of the Research Club, sponsored the
school's first Parent-Teacher Association, taught a
young adult's Sunday school class for years, could

Easter party, 1924, on our front steps.

plan and prepare excellent meals, and grew beautiful flowers.

On the other hand, she considered ironing a waste of time. "Just shake the garment out and walk fast," was her advice. And my older sister used to laugh at watching Mother hurry to the front door to greet company, dusting with her petticoat as she went.

She did enjoy company and was by nature a gracious, thoughtful hostess. That is why I was somewhat surprised at the manner in which she dealt with three uninteresting guests one afternoon.

It was wintertime, not freezing cold but the fire in the living room where we were sitting felt mighty good. The guests had stayed entirely too long, overstayed their welcome as Aunt Bet would say. Conversation had run out, but the trio showed no intention of leaving.

Suddenly Mother arose from her chair and said in a soft but firm voice, "Let's move out onto the porch where it is more pleasant." The guests may have been surprised too, but they departed.

And another saying was added to our family collection.

So many memories scattered through my long life, memories reminding me that one thought, one interesting thought, does indeed lead to another.